Department of the Environment

THE CROWN JEWELS

at the
TOWER OF LONDON

BY MARTIN HOLMES F S A

LONDON

HER MAJESTY'S STATIONERY OFFICE

1968

First published 1953
Third edition 1968
Third impression 1971

Inside front cover: The Coronation of Her Majesty Queen Elizabeth II, 2nd June 1953

Opposite page: The Jewels as displayed about 1820

THE CROWN JEWELS OF ENGLAND

THE treasures of the Jewel House in the Tower of London are, for the most part, connected with the coronation of the kings and queens of England, and almost all are of seventeenth-century and later date. The execution of Charles I in 1649 had been followed by the systematic destruction of the royal ornaments, some of which would seem to have dated from the early Middle Ages, and possibly from the time of Edward the Confessor himself, so that a new set had to be made for the coronation of Charles II in 1661. Since then, additional pieces have been provided from time to time, generally following the earlier forms. The hall-mark on each piece gives the year of its manufacture, but its introduction into the Regalia, or its association with some particular sovereign, may have come at a later date, so that a piece may be stamped with a date-letter somewhat earlier than the accession of the king or queen whose initials it bears.

Processional Objects, Maces

Of the great silver-gilt maces, for instance, two bear the royal cypher of Charles II, two of James II, three of William and Mary and one of Queen Anne, subsequently altered to that of George I. This last mace has no traceable date-marks, but seems by its style to have been made originally for Charles II, whose other maces are likewise undated, most of the later examples bearing the stamp of the noted

The crowning of St. Edmund of East Anglia in 856. From a twelfth-century manuscript from the Abbey of St. Edmund

The Imperial State Crown, worn on State occasions. In front is the
balas ruby given to the Black Prince in the fourteenth century

The head of
the Sceptre
with the Cross

The Sovereign's Orb
and Queen Mary II's Orb

London silversmith, Francis Garthorne. Their shape illustrates how the functions of the fighting-mace were almost forgotten as it developed into the ceremonial staff carried by a king's officer as a sign of his authority, for the great crowned mace-head is an elaboration of the crown and arms that once tipped the butt-end of the shaft, while the true fighting-head with its surrounding flanges has shrunk to a mere fluted knop or pommel. Pairs of these maces are still carried by the Sergeants-at-Arms on certain State occasions; two others, when Parliament is sitting, rest in the Houses of Lords and Commons, and yet another is held by the Lord Chancellor, the senior law officer of the Crown.

Trumpets

In the same way, the set of sixteen State Trumpets has been gradually accumulated over the years. They are all made of silver, the earliest dated from 1780. The hall-marks show that the others came singly at irregular intervals from 1804 to 1813, except for a set of four made in 1813, presumably at the command of the Prince Regent. Ten of them still retain their banners embroidered with the Royal Arms, but unlike the maces the trumpets are now no longer used.

Swords

The three Swords of Justice are borne before the sovereign at a coronation, a custom that can be traced as far back as 1189, when Richard I was crowned, though it is not until 1236, at the coronation of Eleanor, consort of Henry III, that we find the name *Curtana* given to the principal sword of the three. The word is a latinisation of *Courtain*, the name of the short sword of Ogier the Dane, whom twelfth-century legend declared to have been one of the peers of Charlemagne and, for a period, King of England. Ogier was supposed to have drawn Courtain against the son of Charlemagne in revenge for the murder of his own son, but to have been warned by a voice from Heaven to show mercy instead of claiming vengeance. The fact that Matthew Paris, in the thirteenth century, refers to Curtana as the Sword of St. Edward, and that it was traditionally called the Sword of Mercy, suggests an early belief that the actual sword with which Ogier had spared his enemy had been preserved, among the relics of the saintly Confessor, to play its part in the hallowing of those who should come after him.

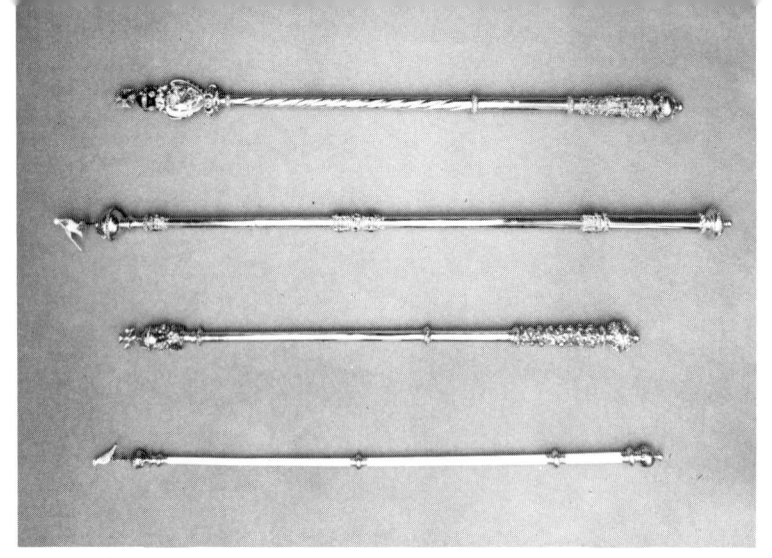

Sceptre with the Cross; Rod of Equity and Mercy;
Queen Consort's Sceptre; Queen Consort's Ivory Rod

The sword seems always to have been short, broad and unpointed, and it would seem that in early coronations it took the part now assigned to the Sword of State. Richard II appears actually to have been girt with it; in the lists of expenses for the coronation of Henry VII we find the cost of purchasing two swords with points and two swords without points called Curtana, while in the document called the 'Little Device' for this coronation (drawn up originally, it would seem, for the coronation of Richard III two years before) it is mentioned that Curtana *and* the sword girt about the king should be 'both flatt w'oute sharpe poyntes', implying that both represent the same sword. The present Curtana has been made blunt and short by breaking off the point of an ordinary double-edged blade of the seventeenth century, which bears the 'running wolf' mark used chiefly by the bladesmiths of Passau and Solingen.

Of the other two Swords of Justice, one bears a similar mark to Curtana's, the other the almost obliterated traces of the bladesmith's name, possibly that Ferrara which appears on so many blades, generally Scottish, of the seventeenth and eighteenth centuries. The two are usually regarded as swords of justice to churchmen and laymen respectively, and probably all three were made for the coronation of Charles II, using old blades which may well have seen service for or against his father in the Civil War. It is worth remembering

Golden Spurs and Bracelets

that before the Reformation the kings of England did not claim jurisdiction in the spiritual courts, and the words 'sword of the church' used by medieval chroniclers such as Wavrin, refer only to the king's function as its champion and defender, bound by his coronation oath to 'protect the holy church of God'. The three swords stood, accordingly, for mercy, justice and the championship of the Church, the three services to which the king's sword had been dedicated when it was first brought to him from the altar.

Larger than these three is the great Sword of State, which represents the sovereign's own personal sword. It is a two-handed sword of the seventeenth century, the quillons of the hilt ingeniously fashioned in the shape of the lion and unicorn that support the Royal Arms. On the grip and pommel are the badges of England, Scotland, France and Ireland, and the portcullis particularly associated with Westminster. All these are repeated on the crimson velvet scabbard, with the addition of the Royal Arms as borne by William and Mary. The records of the Jewel House, however, show that in fact it was provided for Charles II in 1678, the arms of the joint sovereigns being added to it in 1689 to bring it up to date.

At the coronation, the new king or queen enters Westminster Abbey in the robes of a Peer of Parliament, preceded by this Great Sword of State, and by the Swords of Justice and Mercy. In due course, these robes are laid aside for the Anointing, after which their place is taken by the vestments of cloth of gold (as described later) and the imposition of St. Edward's Crown.

Christening Font and Dish

Dish warmer and cover, *c.* 1820

Robes of the
Royal Victorian Order

Robes of the
Order of the Garter

Alms Dish, 1660

Ewer and basin, *c.* 1735

Charles II salt cellar

Elizabeth I salt cellar

Maces carried by
the Sergeants-at-Arms

The use of this name has a significance of its own. One of the most important pledges given by William the Conqueror – a pledge still to be seen in the Guildhall Museum – is his undertaking to the bishop and officers of London to preserve, in all essentials, the constitution of the saint-king Edward the Confessor, whose legal heir William claimed to be. In the next two hundred years, kings were consecrated at Westminster without any special allusion to the Confessor, and their royal ornaments had no association with him by name or tradition: but in 1269 Henry III, who held him in particular veneration, had his bones transferred to a new and splendid shrine, and it is after this that we first hear of the Confessor's relics being used at coronations. The fourteenth-century *Liber Regalis*, still preserved at Westminster, contains a coronation order in which the new king was required to give an undertaking that he would govern in accordance with the old laws of the Confessor, and it seems more than likely that by the end of the thirteenth century certain ancient robes and ornaments, taken from the saint's body at its translation to the present shrine, were actually put upon the king at his coronation. Such an act would serve to indicate his assumption of the crown, the duties and, in some degree, the nature and personality of the monarch whom Englishmen were now regarding as a legendary ideal of kingly goodness.

Even when the actual Saxon diadem 'of gould wyerworke sett with slight stones and two little bells' had been broken under the hammers of the Parliamentary Commissioners, the name and the tradition survived till the Restoration, and the name of St. Edward's Crown is still given to the coronation crown of the kings of England, whatever crown is used for the purpose.

Owing to its great weight – nearly five pounds avoirdupois – St. Edward's Crown is used for the ceremony of coronation only. It is exchanged for the lighter Crown of State at the part of the service known as the Recess, when the newly-crowned monarch retires to the chapel of the Confessor, behind the high altar, and exchanges the golden robes and ornaments of the successor of St. Edward for the purple and diamonds of a sovereign prince. These are worn for the departure from the Abbey and used to be retained for the coronation banquet in Westminster Hall, an elaborate and expensive function last held in 1821 for George IV, but discontinued by his successors.

SACRAMENTAL PLATE

Much of the fine silver-gilt plate now in the Jewel House was provided for use at the coronation banquet, but there are certain early pieces which would appear to have been used at the ceremony itself, notably the chalices and patens of solid gold, engraved with the Royal Arms of William and Mary but obviously of mid-seventeenth-century date. These have sometimes been used for the administration of the Sacraments in the coronation service, and the altar of the Abbey has long been adorned, on such occasions, with the silver-gilt altar-dish and flagon made for William and Mary in 1691 and still used for the same purpose in the Chapel of St. Peter ad Vincula in the Tower on certain festivals of the Church. The altar-dish is decorated with a scriptural scene, apparently the Supper at Emmaus, but the Maundy Dish, displayed nearby, is severely plain, except for the Royal Arms added in the reign of William and Mary, the dish itself being a Restoration piece. Its function is to hold the gifts of money distributed by the sovereign on Holy Thursday at the ceremony of the Royal Maundy. The Maundy money, properly speaking, consists of sets of small silver coins of the value of a penny, twopence, threepence and fourpence, and is still awarded, on certain occasions, as prizes at Westminster School, but the Maundy distributed on Holy Thursday is supplemented by an allowance in modern currency.

Font

The tall covered font and its accompanying dish were made in 1660 by a goldsmith who used the initials R.F. as a signature. From its measurements, the dish would seem to have been originally the wide base on which the font stood, and its elaborate front or lining, apparently of Continental make, used to be detachable, but this is now permanently fixed, and the piece is used as an altar-dish. The first sovereign to be christened in this font was George IV, since Charles II left no legitimate heir, the son of James II never attained the throne, William III and the first two Georges were born and christened abroad, and though George III was born in England, his father was in disgrace at the time and was not tolerated at Court. A silver-gilt ewer and basin, still preserved, were used accordingly at the infant prince's christening, though the Royal Font was brought into use again for most of his own sons and daughters. A smaller

St. Edward's Crown with which the Sovereign is crowned

Ampulla and Spoon

Hilt and scabbard of
the Jewelled State Sword

Great Sword of State
with scabbard

Insignia of
the Order
of the
British Empire

Silver-gilt tankards, *c.* 1661

font, of lily form and suitable for standing on a table, was made in 1840 for the christening of Queen Victoria's children. Two tankards, rather crudely decorated with bacchanalian scenes, have been associated with the earlier font since the eighteenth century, but have no place in the ceremony.

BANQUETING PLATE

The oldest piece of banqueting plate is the so-called Queen Elizabeth's Salt, made in 1572, but there is no record of any personal connection with the queen whose name it bears. Of the other pieces, the two largest were accession-presents to Charles II from two West Country cities, the State Salt being the gift of the city of Exeter, the Fountain that of Plymouth. The State Salt has been described as a model of the White Tower, but bears little resemblance to it, having more in common with some of the elaborate table clocks of the sixteenth century. The square structure like a Norman castle-keep is surmounted by a circular tower reminiscent of a 'drum' clock; above this are an open arcaded gallery equipped with cannon, a dome like the bell of the clock, another arcade, empty this time, and an openwork finial like a crown. The whole piece, including the rocky, lizard-haunted mound on which it stands, is adorned with precious and semi-precious stones.

The gift from the city of Plymouth is nowadays generally known as the Wine Fountain, but this name was given to it only in the last century, and is almost certainly incorrect. The piece appears more likely to have been intended as a source of warm, possibly scented, water in which diners could periodically rinse their cutlery and, if occasion arose, their fingers. The shell-like basins at the feet of the figures round the central column, and the corresponding depressions in the wide, circular platform below, would all be well suited to such a purpose, but it would be impossible to fill wineglasses from them. It may be assumed, then, that the vessel was used for the same purpose as the rose-water dishes that are still handed round at the dinners of certain Livery Companies in the City of London.

The twelve 'St. George's Salts', as they are called, were made at the Restoration and were last used at the coronation banquet of George IV, and the twelve silver-gilt spoons were made for that occasion. Flat dishes were made at the same time to rest on the napkin-brackets of the four pieces that were not intended to have canopies, and the missing canopy of one of the others was replaced by one

Crown worn by George V at the Delhi Durbar in 1911

made in Restoration style, to match its fellows, and surmounted, like them, by an armed and mounted figure, from which the set presumably took its traditional name. An interesting item of banqueting plate, still preserved in the Royal collections, is the *Cadinett*, a case to hold knife, fork and spoon for the King and Queen, placed on the Sovereign's table at the coronation banquet of William and Mary.

THE OLD CROWNS

Some of the coronation ornaments themselves have become obsolete, like the Banqueting Plate, and are preserved for display, but are no longer used in the ceremony. One such piece is the jewelled circlet worn by Mary of Modena, the second wife of James II, when going to her coronation in 1685. It consists of a broad gold band rising slightly in the front and overlaid with jewelled ornaments in settings of thin silver. The velvet cap within it is a modern reconstruction following the proportions of the original. The circlet was apparently worn by successive queens consort in the seventeenth, eighteenth and nineteenth centuries, when its small size was well proportioned to the high hairdressing of the time. However, its use has not been revived in the present century, and its last wearer was Queen Adelaide in 1831. The present setting of the jewels appears to date from the early eighteenth century, and may be part of the work done by Francis Grose, father of the antiquary, for Caroline of Anspach, consort of George II.

Another small crown, no larger than the circlet but surmounted with the usual arches and finial, was Mary of Modena's crown of state, later used as the coronation crown of Queen Anne, and may well have been used – as the jeweller's bills seem to imply – as a crown of state in 1714, to surmount the full-bottomed periwig of George I.

The Prince of Wales's Crown now on display was made in 1729 for Frederick Louis, son of George II. Charles II had sanctioned the heraldic use of the single-arched form to distinguish the coronet of a Prince of Wales from those of the other children of the sovereign, though it was over half a century before the design was actually put into practice.

Queen Victoria had a small diamond crown made, of the heraldic Tudor form, and is shown wearing it in her statue at Windsor and in various late portraits. This crown was for a long time preserved at Windsor, but is now exhibited at the Tower among the other Crown Jewels.

Crown of
Queen Elizabeth
the Queen Mother

Crown of
Queen Mary, Consort
of George V

Table Fountain

Exeter Salt

Altar Dish, 1664

25

The Lily Font

Pitcher, 1692

Candlesticks, *c.* 1662

Chalice, 1664

Queen Victoria's small crown

THE CORONATION REGALIA

Turning to the objects that still play a part in the coronation ceremony, we may remember that the rite, in this country, has long consisted of three main sections. First comes the mutual acceptance of sovereign and people, in which the new king is presented to the congregation for their formal recognition and in his turn takes the Coronation Oath to show that he recognizes and accepts the duties and responsibilities of kingship. Then comes the actual anointing ceremony, in which the sovereign is solemnly consecrated to his high office, followed by his investiture in the various royal ornaments, which includes the delivery of the sword, belt and spurs of knighthood and culminates with the imposition of St. Edward's Crown.

Ampulla and Spoon

The Ampulla and Spoon, the oldest objects among the Regalia, are not themselves royal ornaments, or immediately recognizable as

Crown and diadem of Mary of Modena

being connected with the ceremony, and to that fact, in all probability, they owe their preservation when the more obvious attributes of royalty were destroyed. None the less, they are intimately connected with the most solemn moment of the whole ceremony, when the holy oil, poured from the beak of the golden eagle into the coronation spoon, is applied by the officiating bishop or archbishop to the new sovereign's head, breast and palms. The decoration of the spoon suggests an early date for it, as the handle shows a pattern of strapwork and filigree scrolls characteristic of the late twelfth century. The Ampulla itself is more difficult to date, and its antiquity is less obvious at first sight, since it has been subjected to frequent redecoration, and its feathering is characteristic seventeenth-century work. When its head is removed, however, the comparatively crude threading of the screw at the neck shows that the vessel is far older than its engraved surface suggests, and may well be the golden eagle used for the first time at the coronation of Henry IV in 1399. Probably, in accordance with the fashion of that period, jewels were set in an ornamental cresting round the foot, as may be seen round the Royal Gold Cup in the British Museum.

Sword and Spurs

After the anointing, the monarch is invested with the supertunic, or close pall, of gold brocade, and the individual attributes of knighthood, namely the Sword and Spurs. The golden spurs are no longer actually buckled on, but are applied for a moment to the king's heels and then placed upon the altar. Though made, like so many of the other ornaments, for the coronation of Charles II, they conform to the old pre-Norman type with a single point at the heel instead of a rowel.

The sword is then delivered, to the accompaniment of an impressive exhortation. 'With this sword', says the archbishop, 'do justice, stop the growth of iniquity, protect the holy Church of God, help and defend widows and orphans, restore the things that are gone to decay, maintain the things that are restored, punish and reform what is amiss, and confirm what is in good order.' The new king then ungirds the sword and offers it himself upon the altar, after which it is 'redeemed' for a fee and carried naked before him for the rest of the ceremony. The jewelled sword used for this purpose was made for the coronation of George IV. Its quillons, formed like lions' heads, are thickly encrusted with diamonds, and its grip, pommel and scabbard are of gold, set with jewels in a design incorporating the national emblems of England, Scotland and Ireland.

Armills

The Armills, or 'Bracelets of sincerity and wisdom', which are next put on, are accompanied by an embroidered stole of cloth of gold, which is made anew for each sovereign. It is possible, though not certain, that at early coronations the bracelets were attached to the stole, which thus kept them from sliding down the wearers' arms, and it is probably on this account that the rubrics indicate that the stole should be tied in place with silken laces. The golden bracelets made for the coronation of Queen Elizabeth II in 1953, are lighter, less ornate and easier to wear than those made for Charles II and carried, though not always worn, at the crowning of some, at least, of his successors.

The Orb

The symbolism of the Orb – the globe of the world dominated by the emblem of Christianity – is emphasized by the archbishop when he

The Victoria Cross   The George Cross

puts it into the king's hand after investiture with the Royal Mantle, but it is then handed back, so as to leave both hands free for the Ring and the two Sceptres.

The Ring

The 'ring of kingly dignity' is placed on the third finger of the right hand – the finger on which a wedding-ring used to be worn – and is now a sapphire with the Cross of St. George set on it in rubies. The ring made for William IV was not used for Queen Victoria, who had a smaller one made for her, but her successors were all invested, when their time came, with King William's ring.

Sceptres

The forms of the two royal Sceptres are well known. The Sceptre with the Cross is described, at its delivery, as the 'Ensign of Kingly Power and Justice'. As the Sword has been the token of knighthood, so the Sceptre symbolizes the king's power as the ruler of his people, and the Rod with the Dove his paternal function as their guardian and their guide, since from the earliest times the delivery of the 'Rod

The crown made for the Prince of Wales in 1729

Chalices and patens

Coronation rings

of Equity and Mercy' has been accompanied with the exhortation to the king to guide his people in the way they should go. The Dove, it may be assumed, was symbolic of Divine inspiration, and Montfaucon in 1729 assigned a similar significance to the 'Hand of Justice' of the French kings. In each instance we find two sceptres, one typifying kingly rule and the other bearing a sign of the Divine favour inspiring the 'Lord's Anointed'. This rod shows little trace of recent alteration, but the Sceptre with the Cross has been enriched in the present century with the great diamond, weighing 530 carats, which was the largest of the four 'Stars of Africa' presented by the Government of the Transvaal Colony to King Edward VII. The second of these stones is to be seen in the State Crown, below the cross in the front, and the other two are in the crown of the Queen Consort.

St. Edward's Crown

The last ornament to be delivered is St. Edward's Crown. This, as has been said, is the name traditionally applied to the coronation crown of England, but most properly belongs to the great gold crown made for Charles II and still used for the coronation ceremony. Its shape is characteristic of the period when it was made; the earlier crowns, as can be seen from the portraits of Charles I by Mytens and Van Dyck, were not depressed at the top, and the depression and lateral spread of the present crown are in keeping with the general style of mid-seventeenth-century ornament and the fact that it was made to surmount the long, flowing black curls – not, at that time, a periwig, but the king's own hair – so familiarly associated with Charles II. Recent investigation among the public records has established that the coronation expenses of the time show no charge for the eighty-odd ounces of gold required for its making, and that although the broken gold of the Saxon crown destroyed by the Puritans had been delivered to the Mint to be coined, to the amount of seventy-nine ounces and a half, the surviving records of the Mint show that in each recorded issue of gold coins between the destruction of the Regalia and King Charles's restoration, the metal came in the form of ingots of bullion. Some plate is recorded as having been melted down and sent to the Mint in ingot form, but there is no such entry about St. Edward's Crown, which appears to have been delivered there as scrap metal. It was widely believed, at the time, that the gold crown had really been St. Edward's, and it seems that it may well have been fashioned from the broken metal of the ancient Saxon diadem.

St. Edward's Staff

Another relic of the saint is commemorated in the name of St. Edward's Staff, a long sceptre traditionally carried in the procession though not used in the actual ceremony. This is considerably longer than its fellows, and its golden shaft ends in a steel ferrule, since the original Staff was probably intended as a walking-stick. As early as the reign of Henry VI, however, we hear of it being merely carried as a relic of the Confessor, and the present Staff has been similarly carried to the coronation of Charles II and his successors, though it has no personal association with St. Edward. An interesting point, however, is that it was apparently kept in the Abbey and handed over by the abbot to the sovereign on his entrance, being handed back as the royal procession left the building. Westminster Abbey was and remains a 'Royal Peculiar'; its pre-Reformation abbots owed allegiance to no bishop or archbishop, and it looks very much as if this relic were used as a sign of authority, which the abbot surrendered, as the Lord Mayor of London still formally surrenders the City Sword at Temple Bar, to the one person in England who had the right to take it from him. The custom appears to have survived the Reformation, since we hear of Elizabeth I receiving 'a scepter of gould, having the image of a dove in the toppe', on arriving at the Abbey, and surrendering it on her departure. To this day St. Edward's Staff is laid aside upon the altar of the Abbey after the ceremony, and has no place in the return journey.

Crown of State

The Crown of State, worn for the return from the Abbey and on certain State occasions, is perhaps the best-known crown of all. It was remade with a new frame for King George VI in 1937, still keeping the shape of the coronation crown of Queen Victoria and King Edward VII, the jewels of which were duly transferred to it. Most conspicuous among these are the great irregular spinel called the Black Prince's Ruby, which was traditionally given to that prince in the fourteenth century, and later adorned the helmet-crown of Henry V at Agincourt, and the Stuart Sapphire, almost its equal in size, which was taken away by James II in his flight and remained in the possession of the exiled house of Stuart until the death of Cardinal

Henry Benedict Stuart, the last direct heir. The four long pearl drops below the finial of the State Crown are popularly known as 'Queen Elizabeth's ear-rings', but there is no documentary record of their history, so that the attribution rests on tradition alone.

CONSORT'S REGALIA

When a king's consort is crowned with him, she is given a simpler version of the Sceptre with the Cross, but instead of the Sceptre with the Dove she carries the Ivory Rod. These were both made for the coronation of Mary of Modena, and have been used regularly since then, except in 1689, when Mary II was invested with the Orb and Sceptre with the Dove instead of the Ivory Rod. Mary, as daughter of the deposed James II, was heiress to the throne in her own right, but both she and her husband had insisted, as a condition of his coming to England at all, that he should be considered no mere consort, but should be crowned on terms of absolute equality with her, as King William III. At this coronation, therefore, and this alone, two orbs and sceptres were used, and a replica of the Coronation Chair was made for the Queen's investiture. The Queen's Orb and

Jewels in the Wakefield Tower about 1875

Sceptre are a little smaller than those already described, but resemble them in general appearance. The Consort's Ring now used is that made for Queen Adelaide in 1831, and is set with a single ruby surrounded by diamonds with a band of small rubies round the hoop.

At the beginning of the present century, a slightly different type of arch, of ogival form, was introduced for the crown of Queen Alexandra, and is here exemplified in the coronation crown of Queen Mary and the crown made for the Delhi Durbar of King George V. For many centuries the normal crowns of England have been restricted by statute to the shores of Great Britain, and accordingly a special crown had to be made for the ceremony overseas.

Queen Mary presented her coronation crown, in 1914, to King George V for the use of future queens consort, but at the next coronation she was still present, wearing the diadem without the arches, and a new crown was made for Queen Elizabeth the Queen Mother, and set with diamonds from a circlet that had been worn by Queen Victoria. Conspicuous in this last crown is the famous Indian diamond known as the Koh-i-Noor, or Mountain of Light, the history of which can be traced back to the end of the thirteenth century. It is traditionally supposed to bring good luck to a woman who wears it, but ill-luck to a man, and may be easily recognized in the cross that occupies the front of the crown.

ADMISSION TO VIEW THE CROWN JEWELS
FROM 1 MARCH TO 31 OCTOBER

Weekdays open 9.30 am   *Sundays* open 2 pm

Last ticket sold for admission to:
  Tower of London   5 pm | Tower of London   5 pm
  Jewel House   5.45 pm | Jewel House   5.30 pm

FROM 1 NOVEMBER TO 28 FEBRUARY

Weekdays only open 9.30 am   (not open Sundays)

Last ticket sold for admission to:
  Tower of London   4 pm
  Jewel House   4.30 pm

Closed Christmas Day and Good Friday

SEASON TICKETS, valid for a year from the date of issue, admit their holders to all ancient monuments and historic buildings in the care of the State. Tickets can be purchased at many monuments; at HMSO bookshops; and from the Department of the Environment (AMSS/P), Lambeth Bridge House, London SE1, who will supply full information on request.

Printed in England for Her Majesty's Stationery Office by W. S. Cowell Ltd, Ipswich   Dd 500689   K 2512   6/71